Arnol

with Daybrook aı

on old picture postcards

Ken Negus A.L.A.
Librarian, Arnold Public Library, 1957-74
Gedling District Librarian, 1974-85

FRONT STREET, ARNOLD, NOTTS.

1. Known by local people as Packer's Corner, this 1907 postcard (published by Albert Hindley of Clumber Street) shows its location on the corner of Front Street and Gedling Road, now the Market Place. After Packer left, the shop was taken over by Boots the Chemists. Also on the card are Hopewells, general drapers, and the Central Boot Co., eventually the Northampton Boot and Shoe Co. Note the only vehicle on the street was a milk float.

£2.95

Designed and Published by
Reflections of a Bygone Age
Keyworth, Nottingham
1991

Printed by
Adlard Print and Typesetting Services,
Ruddington, Notts.

ISBN 0 946245 47 9

This book sets out to portray Arnold as it was earlier this century through the medium of picture postcards.

Picture Postcards were first published in Britain in 1894, but it was not until a decade later that they began to take off, when in 1902 the Post Office allowed a message to be written on the address side. This meant that the whole of one side was available for the picture and obviously gave more scope to publishers. Photographic viewcards became very popular, and the postcard became the most important way of communicating news or messages, in much the same way as the telephone is used today. The years up to 1914 were the 'Golden Age' of picture postcards, when millions of imaginative designs covering every subject under the sun were published by a host of national and local firms. There's hardly a village or hamlet that wasn't documented at that time by a postcard publisher, though sometimes the number of cards available was unrelated to the size of a community.

The postcards in this book are the work of eight named publishers though some were produced anonymously. With the exception of W.H. Smith, all the publishers were local. The earliest were issued by Albert Hindley, who ran a stationery shop on Clumber Street, and published the 'Clumber' series of postcards covering much of Nottinghamshire. The two most important Arnold publishers were B.H. Tatham of Church Drive, Daybrook, and R. Beeton of St. Albans Studio, Redhill.

An added bonus of the picture postcard is often the message on the reverse, which can often be relevant to the place the card was posted from.

Back cover: (top) Front Street, Arnold, showing the Maypole and the Meadow Dairy Company, two 'multiple' shops. The Front Street Baptist Chapel and Radfords boot and shoe shop are also in view. These shops were built with two upper storeys so that the families of the owners or managers could live over the premises and not have their living quarters behind the shops. Note the passing loop for the trams. "Rex" series card no. 2128.

Ken Negus would be pleased to hear of any other Arnold and district postcards or photographs not featured in this book, or of any interesting information about Arnold. He can be contacted on Nottingham 264750.

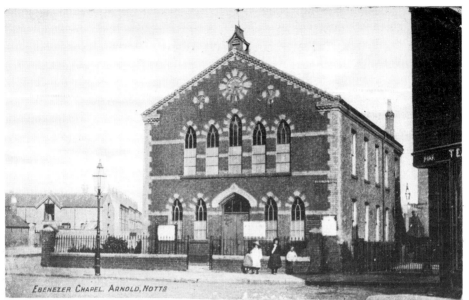

EBENEZER CHAPEL. ARNOLD, NOTTS.

2. Packer's Corner is on the extreme right, with a little of the British National School just showing between it and the Ebenezer, or Front Street Methodist Chapel. This was built in 1865 and was replaced by the present one in September 1967. The clock cost £60, the money being raised by public subscription. On the left on Worrall Avenue are the outbuildings of R. (Bob) Sutton and Sons, who were hay and straw dealers.

"TOP END." ARNOLD.

3. A view from St. Mary's church tower, looking over the old vicarage. In the front is Calverton Road, connected (centre left) by Queen Street to Surgey's Lane, formerly Broad Ass Lane, where the Isolation Hospital can be seen. The house in the right foreground with the two upper storeys is still there. The slope now accommodates Holmefield Avenue, Patricia Drive, Pond Hills Lane, Sunninghill Rise, Upminster Drive and others.

INTRODUCTION

The first mention we have of Arnold is in the Domesday Book of 1086, when the entry noted that the settlement was called Ernehale, which the English Name Place Society notes as meaning *'the place where there are eagles'*. With a population in the region of 100-150 the land under cultivation would be not less than 500 acres and most likely in the area round where St. Mary's Church is now. There was every reason for a settlement being in that area, because all the necessities were to hand for the feeding, clothing and heating of the people. Land would have been cleared for the growing of crops or used for the grazing of cattle and other domestic animals.

Whilst there was no mention of a church in the Domesday Book, we do have one noted in 1176, when a dower ceremony, prior to a marriage service, took place at the church door. A dower ceremony was the giving of monies, lands or cattle, or any mixture of these, to the bridegroom by the bride's father. It is recorded about the wedding, *"Here was a family who took there name from there. refidence at this place. William de Beleu, son of Robert who married Alice the daughter of William de Arnal"*, (note variant spelling of Ernehale). Ernehale had gone through sixteen variations, at least, by 1474, we get the spelling of Arnold as we know it today. We know from church records that John de la Launde from Launde Abbey, between Oakham and Uppingham, was sent to re-build the church at Arnold. He was vicar from 1315-1347. We have reason to believe that in his re-building, the only part of the original church to survive is a section of the north wall. Since his time, there have been subsequent additions and alterations.

Very little was recorded about Arnold prior to the sixteenth century but this was altered by an important piece of legislation. A royal proclamation was made in 1538 that a record must be kept of all baptisms, marriages and burials. The first such record in Arnold was of a baptism on 20th November 1544.

The most recent alteration to St. Mary's Church was in 1958-59, when the Coal Board cleared the inside of the church. They then made a concrete raft under the church to allay any possible subsidence, which might arise from the extraction of coal from underneath.

Arnold grew very slowly through the years due to many causes; for instance it is not on a river, main roads, canal or main-line railway and there were very few factories until a hundred years ago. The main employment until then was on the land and frame work knitting, with the frames being chiefly in the homes of the workers. Arnold could be said to have been a self-contained community. With a population of 7,769 in 1891 we find that the houses on Front Street outnumbered the shops and that nearly all the shop-keepers and trades people lived on the premises. These shops and trades included a tailor, shoe-maker, dress-makers, blacksmiths and, of course, butchers and grocers, of whom there were eighteen of the former and thirty-two of the latter in the Arnold area at that time.

What a difference today on Front Street, there being only one private house left, with a greater diversity of shops with such 'new' ones as electrical and motor accessory outlets. In addition we get banks, building societies, dentists, estate agents, solicitors, stationers, travel agents, with many other types of shops and services, not forgetting the many car parks.

Ken Negus
September 1991

Acknowledgement: the majority of postcards in this book come from the Grenville Jennings collection. The publishers and author thank him very much for permitting their use.

4. What a quiet road it was at Redhill prior to the coming of motor vehicles – the cyclists can even ride on the right-hand side of the road. This postcard – and the next one – shows the second bridge, which was put up in 1886. The original road still goes to the right of the present one out of Redhill: it must have been quite a struggle in bad weather to get over the hill. Postcard published by Albert Hindley as no. 19 in his "Clumber" series, with the message on the reverse *"Today the weather could not have been better: we played golf on Bulwell Forest Common."*

5. W.H. Smith card no. 322. The first bridge, made of stone, was built, and the cutting excavated, in 1815 by the nearly-destitute framework knitters who, because of poor trade, a wet harvest, and financial problems, were paid in kind. When the reservoir was being made on Redhill in 1872, the carts with their loads of clay and bricks caused the bridge to crack, hence the need for a replacement. In 1927-8 the road was widened from 22 to 33 feet and the third bridge erected. During 1946 the cutting retaining wall was added, and in 1956 – due to subsidence causing cracks – was buttressed. The present, or fourth, bridge was put in position in April 1985.

6. C. & A.G. Lewis published this card (no. 2778) of the 'Ram Inn' on Mansfield Road. Beyond is the 'Waggon and Horses', and further on the 'Forest Guide House', demolished in 1977 and at one time a coaching inn. On the opposite side was originally another inn, the 'Three Crowns'.

7. Redhill (not Daybrook, as captioned on this 'Peveril' series card) Cemetery was opened in 1879 and enlarged in 1914, by when St. Mary's churchyard was beginning to get full. When it opened, there were two chapels, one on either side of the arch, one for Church of England members, one for 'other denominations'. Card postally used from Arnold in October 1906.

8. There has been a public house on the 'White Hart Hotel' site since the mid-eighteenth century; a sale notice of c.1820 proclaimed "a great house of call for travellers to and from the North." When R. Beeton of St. Albans Studio, Arnold, published this card about 1910, the landlord was George Stockdale, late gamekeeper to the Duke of St. Albans, a one-time owner. Another owner was Mr. James Acton. A new 'White Hart' has taken the place of this building, which was demolished in 1966.

9. Hammond's of Daybrook now stands on this site on the left, started in 1873 by John Lee as a wheelwright, carriage builder and funeral director. It was taken over by Samuel Hammond in September 1905. The row of cottages was on the corner of Oxclose Lane, formerly Basford Lane, where Theodore Dyer, painter and decorator, had a shop.

DAYBROOK CHURCH, NOTTS

10. A view unlikely to be repeated, with horse-drawn vehicles on Mansfield Road. The consecration ceremony at St. Paul's was on Tuesday 4th February 1896, with Rev. E.M. Vaughan as the first vicar. The church cost £20,000 to build, and Sir Charles Seeley was the chief benefactor. Of particular note in the church is the alabaster reredos at the back of the high altar, with its portrayal of the last supper. On the left, just visible, is the 'Old Spot Inn'. "Clumber" series card, posted from Arnold in April 1906.

Church & Alms Houses, Daybrook, Nott's. Peveril Series 702.

11. A similar view, showing the almshouses as well as St. Paul's, the interior of which is faced with Bulwell stone. The almshouses were built in 1899 by Sir John Robinson of the Home Brewery and Daybrook laundry, in memory of his son John Sandford Robinson, an amateur jockey who was killed on 21st April 1898 while horse-racing. The postcard was sent from Arnold in December 1916, with the message *"we came to live here end of July; we are so comfortable, we like it very much."*

New Year's Greetings from YOUR "LAUNDRY MAIDS" AT DAYBROOK.

OUR AIM IS TO SERVE YOU.

DAYBROOK NOTTS. phone: 68256 (2 LINES)

12. Interior view of the Daybrook Laundry, showing household and personal linen being laundered. Today, dry and industrial cleaning work is done here. The Laundry began in 1887 and was built for the Robinsons, who owned the Home Brewery, opened in 1880, across the road. A 1900 advertisement for the Laundry read *"Launderers, Art Dyers, Dry Cleaners, Curtain dressers."*

COTTAGES, DAYBROOK, NOTTS. 372

13. Known as Pleasant Row, these cottages show examples of framework knitters' windows, of which there were many in Arnold at one time. On this site now is Coronation Buildings (referring to that of King George VI and Queen Elizabeth), a group of shops built in 1937. The 'Old Spot' public house can be seen far left. "Clumber" series card no. 372.

14. Daybrook Infants Group III in an unspecified year, probably about 1908. The school was built in 1879 for infants and juniors, with places for 300 children, in a two-storied building. It's now occupied by a petrol filling station on Mansfield Road and Morley Street. No doubt the pupils were dressed in their Sunday best for this photograph.

DAY BROOK FIRE.

15. Jacoby's lace manufacturers, bleachers and dressers factory on Sherbrook Road opened in 1883-4, employing around 300 people. There was a fire at the factory on two occasions, the first on 24th March 1913, featured on this anonymously-published photographic card. The second, in October 1939, caused quite a stir because a number of local people saw the smoke, heard the fire engines, and thought bombs had been dropped on the factory!

16. Daybrook Square. Morley's hosiery factory is in the distance, with a tram emerging at the entrance to Nottingham Road. Moving to the right, we see Steeples, a men's outfitters, Arnot Hill Café, and G. & C. Whittles, painting contractors, who later moved into purpose-built offices and workshops round the corner in Nottingham Road, now occupied by Gedling Borough Council Technical Services Department. On the right is Daybrook Baptist Chapel, built in 1912, and the second on this site: the original was erected in 1859.

17. A letter 'K' tram in Daybrook Square at the junction of Nottingham Road and Mansfield Road. The first tram to Arnold ran on Friday 1st January 1915, Sherwood Depot having been the previous nearest tram terminus. The service lasted 21 years: on Sunday morning, 6th September 1936 at 12.10 a.m. the last tram in Nottingham ran from Daybrook Square to the Old Market Square. Alderman J. Farr J.P., of the Home Brewery was the driver. On the extreme right was a petrol filling station, owned by the son of Samuel Dove *(see illus. 20)*. Later the Midland Bank had a branch built to the left.

18. 'Peveril' series postcard no. 4118, posted from Daybrook in May 1916. I. and R. Morley's factory, Daybrook Square, originally Messrs. Hardys, was sited between Nottingham Road, Morley Street and Mansfield Road, and built in 1885 (the date stone is still over the entrance gate). Originally 560 workers were employed, and an extension, on the right, was added in 1911. Note the boy pushing a wheelbarrow in the middle of the road!

19. Another view of Daybrook Square (on a "Clumber" postcard with April 1906 postmark) looking north towards St. Paul's Church in the middle distance and Sherbrook Road on the left. The shop on the corner was one of the many fish and chip shops in Arnold (in 1946 there were 26!). The double-fronted shop belonged to Fleet the furnishers, funeral directors, and cabinet makers.

20. Looking from Nottingham Road onto Mansfield Road, Daybrook Square, and the 'Grove' Hotel (mine host was W.M. Foster) about 1905. The next shop was owned by newsagent F.W. Alvey. The proprietor of the 'Supply Stores' shop on the left was local councillor Samuel (Sammy) Dove who, among other things, was a furnisher, furniture remover, funeral director, grocer and sub-postmaster. Note the lamp in the middle of the road junction.

21. A longer perspective of the previous view with, at the far left, the Daybrook railway bridge and Station Road going off right to the station. The caption on this postcard published in 1911 by local photographer R. Beeton actually refers to a Sunday School Demonstration.

22. Also by Beeton, this card features one of Dove's delivery vehicles *(see caption to illus. 20),* with solid tyres and carbide head lamps. What an uncomfortable ride it must have been for the driver and his mates, who would at least get plenty of fresh air! Note the telephone number, Arnold 17.

23. *"Daybrook station for Arnold"* was the porter's call. The first train ran in September 1875 and the last on 12th March 1962. This 'back' line ran from Bulwell to Netherfield Junction on the Great Northern Railway and was known as the 'District' Line. On Monday 2nd December 1899 the Nottingham suburban line opened, joining the above line a little along the track into Woodthorpe, near the signal box seen in the distance. "Clumber" series card no. 124.

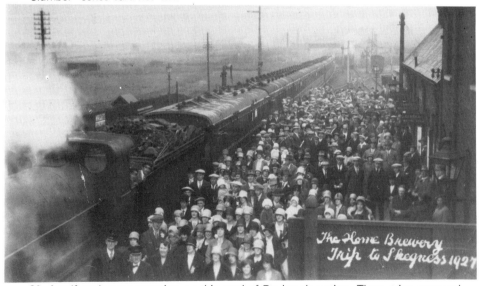

24. A self-explanatory caption on this card of Daybrook station. These trips occurred for a number of years and may have been the only occasion when some of the workers had a day away from Arnold. As late as 1958 there were posters on Station Road approach stating *"Evening trips to Skegness, 2s 6d"* (12½p). In 1910, a journey from Nottingham Victoria to Daybrook via London Road High Level, Thorneywood, St. Anns Well and Sherwood took 17 minutes (13 minutes direct with no stops). A journey on the 'District' line via Netherfield and Gedling lasted 21 minutes.

25. It's difficult to recognise this as the Valley Road playing fields, at one time part of Arnold Urban District before being sold to Nottingham Council. This is where the Daybrook split, going straight on to Edwards Lane, reached via climbing Jacob's Ladder, and the left fork going to what was the city's A.R.P. headquarters during the Second World War – now it's covered by the Five Ways Hotel and Larwood Grove. "Clumber" series card no. 393, posted at Arnold in August 1920.

26. On the right is the 'Black Swan Inn', whose origins can be traced back to 1778 (this building dates from 1808). It stood on Mansfield Road and the corner of the future Villiers Road, shown here as a cart track going off to the left, and developed between 1904 and 1908. This hostelry had many innkeepers including Cockayne, Bostock, Beardsley and finally John Porter, who was also a market gardener. The inn was demolished in 1906.

Woodthorpe Drive Notts.

27. A view of Woodthorpe Drive, formerly Scout Lane, with Woodthorpe Avenue going off to the left and Grange Road in the middle distance. Woodthorpe Park is on the right, with the bridge over the Suburban Railway where the road disappears to the right. "Clumber" series no. 377.

Arno Vale, Notts.

28. Further up Thackeray's Lane from the view in illus. 29 is this cottage, the gatehouse to Arno Vale House, and situated on the right near where the present houses start. "Clumber" no. 396.

THACKERAY'S LANE,
ARNOLD, NOTTS.

29. Another card by the same publisher, postally used in August 1917, showing the bridge on the Suburban Railway over Thackeray's Lane, demolished in 1973. Today Buckingham Road is on the right and there is a roundabout where five roads meet just past where the bridge stood.

ARNO VALE HOUSE ARNOLD.

30. Arno Vale House was between Thackeray's Lane (note the trees in the background), Saville Road and Arno Vale Road. Originally built about 1800, its most well-known occupier was John Lawson Thackeray (hence the lane's name), mayor of Nottingham in 1854 and 1866. Among other occupiers were Rev. Biddle, Mrs. Bigsby, Charles Sneath and Horace Fisher. The latter's daughters were the last occupiers (they gave their name to Fisher Avenue). The house was demolished in July 1935. This Edwardian postcard was published by B.H. Tatham in the "Church" series.

31. The buildings on this card are Arno Vale Farm, formerly Swinehouse Farm, which with the footpath and stile are mentioned in D.H. Lawrence's *Sons and Lovers*. This view was to change quite drastically in the 1920s and 1930s when building started in this part of Woodthorpe. The photographer had his back to Mapperley Plains with Breck Hill Road (just off the photograph) to the left. Long Acre now approximates to the footpath, as does Coningsby Gardens East and Coningsby Road, with the hedge almost being the boundary of Maitland Avenue and Melbury Road. This area was known as Hilly Fields and was a well-used sledging slope.

32. This is a better view of the farm, seen on the previous card. The pond was one of two close to the farm which were noted for their frogs and newts. The last occupiers of the farm were the Chambers family, who came from Hagg's Farm at Eastwood in 1911. The buildings, which stood near the ends of Coningsby Road, Wensley Road and Whernside Road, were demolished about 1933.

33. A Sunday School Demonstration – very common on postcards in the first dozen years of this century – on a card published by B.H. Tatham. This time the crowd is at the end of Nottingham Road and on the site of the future Jubilee Street and fire station. Morley's factory is off the picture to the left, and the entrance to Arnot Hill Park is in the middle distance.

34. Postcard no. 313 in the 'Rex' series, of Arnot Hill Park, postally used in October 1931. From about 1790-1810 a five storey mill stood here; the lake was a man-made mill pond. A thousand people were employed at one period. The mill went bankrupt and could not be sold; a sale notice of 3rd January 1811 said it had been pulled down and the bits and pieces were for sale.

35. Arnold Council, formed from the local Board of Health in 1894, bought Arnot Hill House and grounds, with the object of turning the house into council offices and the grounds into a public park. On 10th August 1914 a deposit of £100 was put towards the total cost of £3,000, or £250 per acre. Note the boat on the lake. Postcard by R. Beeton, posted in August 1920.

36. On 14th September 1914, Arnold Council placed the house at the disposal of the Red Cross Society for the war wounded to convalesce, and it was used for this purpose until 10th March 1919. It is worth noting that at their April 1919 meeting, the council increased the rate by 25% to 2s 5d (12p) *(for further details, see my book 'Arnold Urban District Council 1894-1974).* 'Rex' series postcard no. 315, sent in August 1924. *"Arrived safely. Spent afternoon at Trent Bridge."* The war memorial lists all the Arnold men killed in the Great War.

37. A B.H. Tatham card published about 1905, showing the newly-opened Co-op. The photo was taken from the site of the future St. Albans Picturedrome. The Co-op opened in 1904 and had departments for footwear, haberdashery, groceries and butchery, with stables and a coach-house to the rear. The notice-board on the right is on the site of the future public library.

38. The public library has replaced the notice-board; B.H. Tatham's "Church" series card shows the opening ceremony on Saturday 27th October 1906. It was a closed access library, as were all early libraries, and books had to be chosen from a catalogue in the entrance hall, the librarian fetching the books from the shelves. First librarian at Arnold was James Holbrook.

39. "Clumber" series card of 1906, with a view of the beginning of Front Street. Monk's drapers shop is in the centre, and St. Albans Road, previously called Broadmere Lane, off to the left.

FRONT STREET, ARNOLD, NOTTINGHAM.

40. A postcard published by W.H. Smith about 1913, though not used until July 1917. It features St. Albans Picturedrome, later to be called the 'Bonington', on the right. This opened on Boxing Day in 1912. The tram tracks have not yet been laid, and people can safely stand in the road for the photograph. Talkies came to the cinema on Boxing Day 1931 and the final programme was on 30th March 1957.

Carnegie Library, Arnold, Nottingham.   Rex Series:- No. 192

41. On the left of the library can be seen the fire bell, rung to notify the fire brigade, all part-timers, when they were required. The notice-board on the right corner lists men who were killed in the 1914-18 war. "Rex" series postcard no. 192, posted from Arnold in July 1922, four years before the swimming and slipper baths were built on the extreme right.

42. A very busy scene *(compare illus. 39)* with a number 9 tram running on the Arnold-Sherwood-Old Market Place-Trent Bridge service. The '9' was replaced by the letter 'K' in 1933. At the far end of the library can be seen the tram shelter. "Rex" series postcard no. 191.

ARNOLD, NOTTINGHAM.
REX SERIES - 191.

43. Anonymously-published card of the junction of High Street, formerly Back Street, and Front Street, about 1920. *'Arnold Sq.'*, the caption, must have been applied by a non-local! On the left is one of the early 'multiple' shops, Marsdens, and the white-fronted shop is Kirks the butchers. The Liberal Club is next to it on the corner of West Street. Also in this stretch were Hannah Showell (haberdasher), Frederick Parker, and James Cliff (hairdresser and newsagent). The two shops at the junction are Roberts the hairdresser and Ellis the butcher. A two-storey building on High Street on the right was Harold W. Brailsford's, a general store and pawnbrokers.

Front Street, Arnold.

44. A further view on a W.H. Smith postcard of the beginning of Front Street with a tram near the Ebenezer Chapel. Note how the tram tracks go from double to single. Front Street was narrow in parts, so there were single tracks and passing loops.

45. Frances Skerritt, newsagent, advertises the *News of the World* for 1d. During the first world war, this shop had the only telephone in the area, so was very much in demand. Next door he had a hairdresser's shop, while further on at 29 Front Street was J.W. Ellis, baker. At 31 came Chambers' butcher shop. On the right featured here is Sulleys (baker), Schofield (fish and chips). Earlier, this latter building had been the first telephone exchange in Arnold, a Mrs. Field being in charge. "Rex" series postcard no. 193.

46. A 1950s view of Front Street *(compare top illus., back cover)* with the trams no longer running and some houses on the left demolished, giving a clear view of Shentalls shop. The shop on the right at no. 64 has been in its time a sweet shop, funeral parlour, and a part-time branch of the Midland Bank. Beyond that come Mrs. Andrews, haberdasher, Butterworths, grocer and provision merchant, and then a shop kept by Mrs. Clay. Postcard published by A.W. Bourne of Leicester.

47. "Clumber" series postcard no. 252 of Front Street, incorrectly captioned by the publishers. On the left are Sycamore Villas, where at one time there was a farm. Beyond them are the first council offices, built in 1874 for £979 for the local Board of Health, the forerunners of Arnold Council. There was a public weighbridge in front of this building.

48. A letter 'K' tram at the terminus at the end of Front Street about 1935. On the extreme left can be seen the 'Plough and Harrow' Inn, next to Stone's wallpaper and paint shop on the corner of Church Street and Coppice Road (formerly Spout Lane).

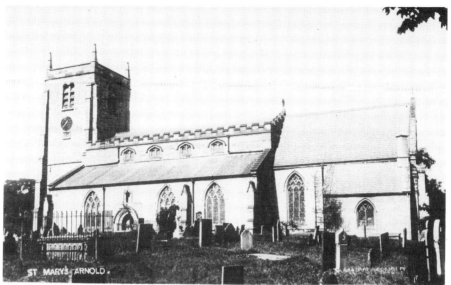

49. St. Mary's Parish Church, known as 'top church', on a card by B.H. Tatham published early this century. The clocks on three sides of the tower were put there in 1868 for just over £161. The present south porch was not added until 1930. *(for a fuller description of the church and its history see my book 'St. Mary's Church, Arnold', available from the church.)*

50. Grove Estate, the first large Arnold council housing development, was built on this site in 1926. It was so called because the area was originally occupied by Grove House, owned by Alderman Robert Mellors, after whom a school and adjacent road was named at the same time as the estate. Any walker from Nottingham Road to Calverton Road had the choice of two routes – via Front and Church Streets, or by High Street, Cross Street, along part of Redhill Road, onto Allen's Walk (seen here), then past the church. "Clumber" series card no. 305, posted at Long Eaton in July 1910.

51. Allen's Walk passed by St. Mary's tower and through the graveyard, coming out alongside the house by the first banner, onto Calverton Road, originally Lane. On the left is the wall which is the vicarage boundary. Beyond the house is the 'Seven Stars' public house, demolished in 1968. On the right is the wall and entrance belonging to Calverton Road school. Another Tatham postcard.

52. B.H. Tatham contributed many postcards of the pre-1914 Sunday School Demonstrations. These took place most years on Whit Tuesday afternoon, though in the 1960s Whit Saturday became the usual date. Here we see a display that was devised by one of the nine chapels (it was only the nonconformists who took part in the Demonstrations). Starting from their place of worship, they paraded through Arnold to a central meeting place – here the Flower Show Field, now the King George V playing field. In later years they went to Nottingham Road Recreation Ground, known as the 'bottom rec.'.

ARNOLD WAKES NOTTS.

53. Not too many years ago, Arnold folk could look forward to the Wakes in September, the festivity nicely spaced out in the year from the demonstrations. The Wakes were really part of the Patronal Festival at St. Mary's Church, commemorating the Nativity of the Virgin Mary, held on the Sunday following 19th September. The fair, just prior to Nottingham's Goose Fair, was held on the Flower Show Field, then Worrall Avenue, then the Croft (the area around Croft Road), and finally on Coppice Road. Card by Tatham, posted at Leicester in October 1907.

54. Another Tatham 'demonstration' card. Each chapel had its own banner (note the names on those shown); the roads were closed off, a practice that continued up to the late 1960s. Virtually everyone on this card is wearing a hat, as was customary eighty years ago.

55. Trams were used for many special events, including the Coronation of George V, when they were decorated and ran to various parts of the system. Another event in Arnold was for children's outings, when a tram was used to take 'poor children' into the city for special treats.

56. Lack of petrol forced this Birdling plane in a *Daily Mail* air race to land in Little Lime Lane, off the Ollerton Road, on 28th July 1911. It got airborne again the next day. Local photographer Tatham published this card.

57. Arnold and District Rifle Club in 1900, with the individual trophy winners listed on the right. President was Lord Osborne Beauclerk, who became the 12th Duke of St. Albans. All are wearing a waistcoat with the usual watch-chain.

58. Card by R. Beeton of Belgian refugees at Arnold. Many were brought to England when war broke out in August 1914 and were housed and cared for in many parts of the country.

59. Any record of Arnold would be incomplete without reference to the various football teams. Here we have Arnold St. Mary's Football Club, Cup Winners in 1908-9. In the 1960s the club changed its name to Arnold Town.